Super Sun Science

Elizabeth Tarski

Rigby

A Harcourt Achieve Imprint

www.Rigby.com
1-800-531-5015

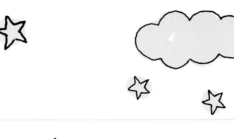

My class had a science unit all about the sun.

I knew that the sun is a star, but I never realized there were so many super things about the sun!

I decided that my science report would be about the sun.

The sun is important for every living thing on our planet. It gives us warmth and light. It's hotter than anything on Earth. Without the sun, Earth would freeze!

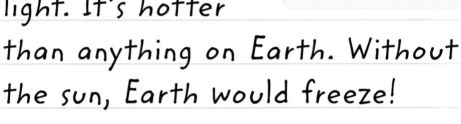

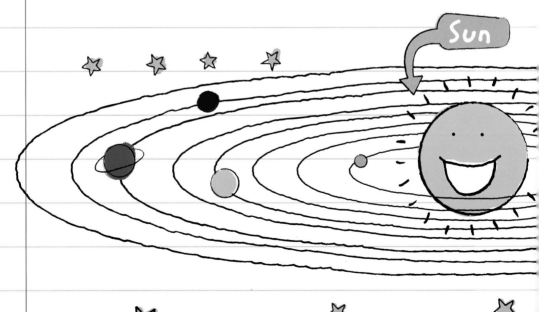

Sun

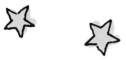
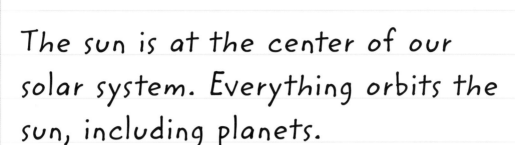

The sun is at the center of our solar system. Everything orbits the sun, including planets.

I found out the sun is very big. It makes up 98% of everything in our solar system.

Objects in the Solar System

98% Sun

2% Other

Earth

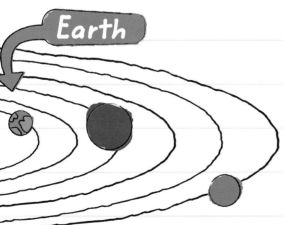

I also learned about sunspots. Sunspots look like dark patches on the sun. Sunspots continue to appear, change position, and disappear on the sun's surface.

X-Ray Photo

In class we looked at pictures of sunspots. Some of the pictures were taken with special scientific cameras. They make the sun look amazing!

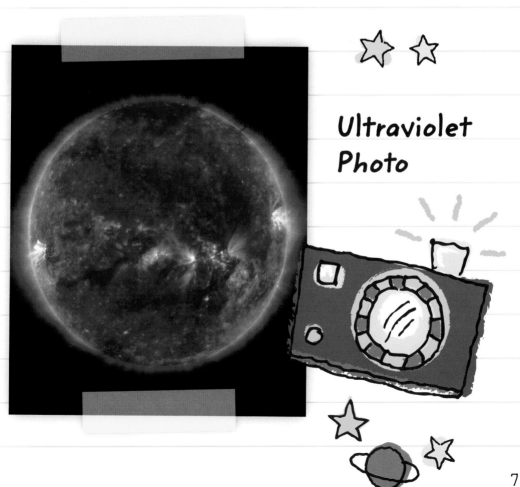

Ultraviolet Photo

I thought sunspots would be small. They look tiny against the sun's surface.

This SUNSPOT is **13** TIMES LARGER than Earth!

 Earth

It turns out that sunspots are huge! Our class looked at a photo of one sunspot as big as 13 Earths. That sunspot would have made Earth look very small!

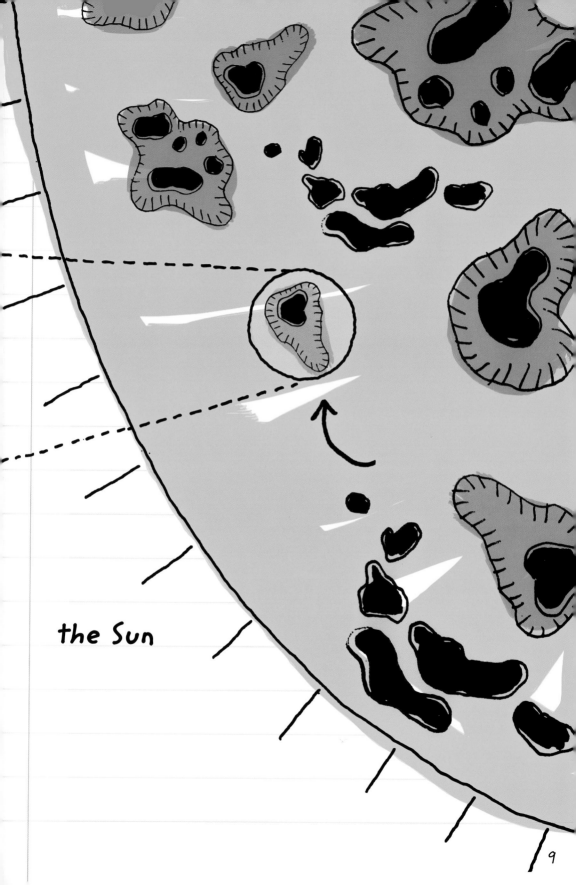

the Sun

Sunspots come and go in cycles. About every 11 years, the sun creates many sunspots in a short time. During this period, you can see more sunspots than at any other time. The last time this happened was in 2001.

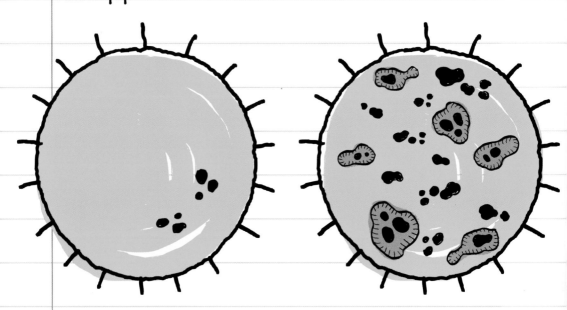

Low Cycle   High Cycle

Scientists know a lot about sunspot cycles. They can even guess how many sunspots will be seen during a cycle. I want to be a sun scientist when I grow up!

Our class went outside to get a look at actual sunspots. We were just like real scientists!

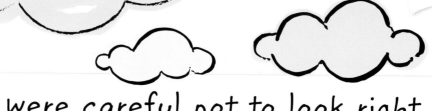

We were careful not to look right at the sun. It is too powerful and bright. We had to block out some of the sunlight or it could have really hurt our eyes!

Our teacher said we could use
a telescope to study sunspots
without hurting our eyes.
But we wouldn't look into
the telescope. We would use
it to create a sun picture.

Our teacher showed us how to set up the telescope to keep our eyes safe. First we pointed the telescope up to the sun.

sunlight

telescope

STEP 1

We put a square piece of cardboard around the telescope's eyepiece. This created a shadow behind the eyepiece.

STEP 2

eyepiece

shadow
cardboard

Next we held a piece of white cardboard close to the eyepiece. The sunlight came through the telescope and made a circle of light on the cardboard. It was like a sun picture!

STEP 3

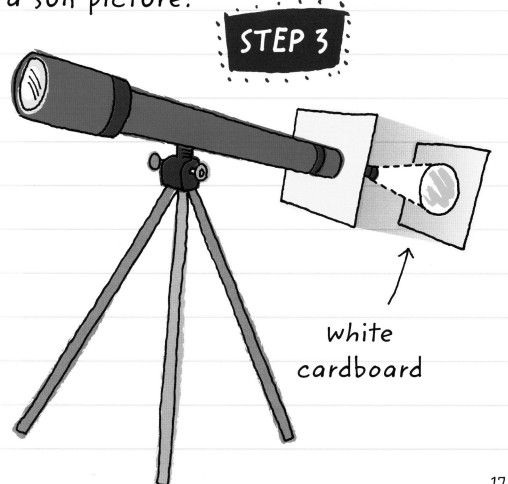

white cardboard

We moved the white cardboard until the sun was in focus. Suddenly, the sunspots became clear. We could see the surface of the sun! It was an easy and safe way to look at sunspots.

STEP 4

Image in Focus

19

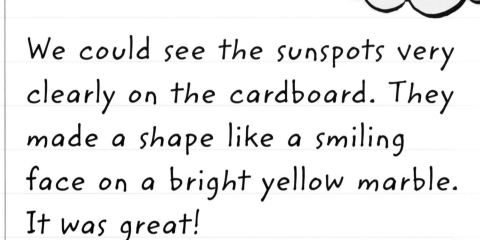

We could see the sunspots very clearly on the cardboard. They made a shape like a smiling face on a bright yellow marble. It was great!

Once we had seen the image of the sunspots, we got to draw and label them on a sunspot chart. Here's what I saw!

Sunspot Observation

Name: Elizabeth   **Date:** April 6, 2007

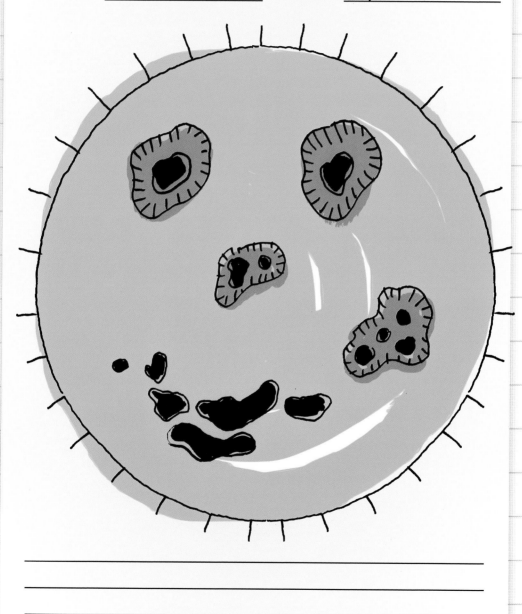

Super Cool Things About the Sun

- More than 1 million Earths would fit inside the sun.

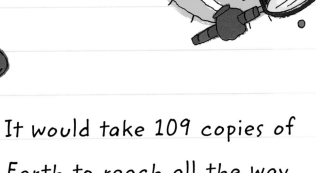

- It would take 109 copies of Earth to reach all the way across the middle of the sun.

- The sun's surface is about 52 times hotter than a pot of boiling water.

- It takes Earth one day to make one rotation. It takes the sun 25 days. That's almost a month!

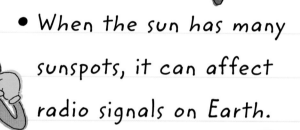

- When the sun has many sunspots, it can affect radio signals on Earth.

- The sun is 400 times bigger than the moon, but it is 400 times farther from Earth. That makes the sun and moon look about the same size in the sky.

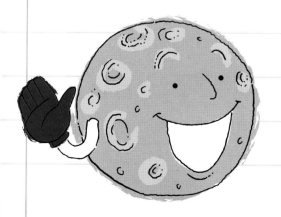

GLOSSARY

orbit to move in a curved path around the sun or a planet

rotation a turn or spin in one place

solar system the sun and all the planets that orbit it, including Earth

telescope a tool that makes things look nearer and larger when you look into it